THOUGHT CATALOG BOOKS

Inside The Heart Of A Strong Woman

Inside The Heart Of A Strong Woman

THOUGHT CATALOG

THOUGHT CATALOG BOOKS

Brooklyn, NY

THOUGHT CATALOG BOOKS

Copyright © 2016 by The Thought & Expression Co.

First edition, 2016

ISBN 978-1535579971

10 9 8 7 6 5 4 3 2 1

Cover photography by © Julia Caesar

Contents

1

15 People Explain What It Means To Be A Strong Woman

Marisa Donnelly

1. She fights against expectations.

"A strong woman has an awareness of the obstacles in her way and the misogynistic expectations people have for her, but she decides for herself what she wants and works to achieve it. Furthermore, a strong woman is willing to find help or gain strength from supportive friends, family members, and mentors—despite the notion that women should be 'independent' and 'do it all.'"

2. She bounces back.

"A strong woman keeps going on like she has never been hurt, despite having been."

3. She knows who she is.

"A strong woman is self-aware. She continually tries to overcome her fears, she knows how to control herself, and she is patient no matter the situation. She isn't afraid to reveal her feelings because we all have them, and she shows hers without caring what other people think."

4. She is independent, but knows when to ask for help.

"Being a strong woman doesn't mean you can't ask for help. Hell, being a strong man doesn't mean you can't ask for help. Part of me thinks that women feel they have to overcompensate because so many peg them as these fragile, helpless creatures, when many of the women I know are stronger (be it mentally, emotionally, or physically) than many of the men I know."

Being a strong woman in my eyes means you're someone who is realistic enough to know what you can do, is grounded enough to know when you need a hand, and is confident enough to know you can ask for help without fear of being judged."

5. She follows her own path.

"A strong woman is someone who follows her own dreams rather than a man."

6. She is unapologetic about who she is.

"A strong woman works hard, she chases what she believes in, and she does it all for herself. No one else. She loves endlessly and shows appreciation to those around her. Most importantly, she isn't selfish, and once she makes it, she reaches back to help others."

7. She's a fighter.

"A strong woman is a woman who fights for rights she shouldn't have to fight for."

8. She's perseverant.

"A strong woman gets up every time she falls. She pushes forward, even when all odds are against her. She doesn't let others influence her decisions. She's resilient."

9. She is balanced.

"A strong woman knows when to be selfish and when to be selfless, when to follow her head and when to follow her heart. She has a good, stable head on her shoulders, and she knows when to play the hand she's dealt and when to fold and hope the next one's better."

10. She doesn't let others define her.

"A strong woman is a busy, vibrant, and goal-orientated woman who doesn't wait for a man to validate her existence."

11. She is grounded in her faith.

"A strong woman believes in whatever she believes in, and lets that faith guide her every step."

12. She isn't afraid to be true to her feelings.

"A strong woman is someone who isn't afraid to share her opinions and speak her truth. She listens, but she doesn't allow others problems to bring her down.

She is filled with kindness, generosity, compassion, integrity, a willingness to be vulnerable, and authenticity. No matter what she is true to herself."

13. She respects herself.

"A strong woman doesn't let the cattiness of other women bring her down. She has the utmost respect for herself and what she believes in."

14. She is humble.

"A strong woman is confident, yes. But I think the best way to describe a woman's strength is a sense of 'confident humility,' paired with faith and passion. By 'confident humility' I just mean someone that isn't so humble that she comes across as weak. Rather, someone that can stay confident without getting arrogant."

15. She loves.

"A strong woman loves inherently, from the time she is a little girl to the day she passes. She is always willing to take care of others. She loves. And never stops loving."

2

This Is How You Date A Strong Woman

Lauren Jarvis-Gibson

A strong woman is a not a force to be reckoned with. She is more real than kind but also more kind than most people you will ever meet. She knows what she deserves and she knows exactly how she should be treated. **So to date a strong woman, you also must be strong.**

A strong woman wants to always be treated with respect. You don't have to give her a dozen red roses on Valentine's Day. You don't have to woo her with sweet handwritten poems, and you don't even have to give her anything for her birthday.

But you better be damn sure that you tell her what she means to you. You better be damn sure you always let her know that she is never alone, even if she tries to put up a wall between you two.

To date a strong woman, you need to be able to man the f**k up. With all the cracks her heart has endured through the years, she has turned it into steel. You need to break down those barriers and see what's inside. **You need to be able to hear her story and not run. You need to be able to hold her**

hand through the times when she doesn't seem so strong anymore and through the times when she is flying on top of the world. Never stop vocalizing to her about how she makes you feel. You don't have to put rose petals on the ground to do this. You don't even need to give her a diamond ring on her shaking finger.

You just need to say it loud and proud, without any hesitation.

Because although she is strong and mighty, she is also human. And humans can break. Humans can hurt. And humans can have trouble feeling like they are never good enough.

She just wants to be enough for you. She wants to make you happy and to see you smile when she kisses you out of the blue. She just wants to make your heart beat a little faster when you see her driving in your driveway. She just wants the little reminders that she is enough.

She needs to know that she is always enough. To date and to love a strong woman, you need to validate this need. You need to step up your game, forget your ego, and give her reassurance that she is beautiful. She doesn't need to play pretend for you or put on pounds of makeup. She doesn't need to make you chocolate covered strawberries on Valentine's Day or squeeze into a little black dress for your anniversary.

And when you finally realize that you are falling for her, please don't hide. Don't run away. Don't be scared. **Just say it. Because when you tell a strong woman you love her, she will**

believe you. And you better be damn sure you do, because if you break a strong woman's heart, she won't give you a second chance.

And she will always know that she is worth so much more than a false whisper of "I love you."

3

10 Reasons Why It's Harder For Strong Women To Find Love

Rania Naim

1. They do not settle.

Strong women have high standards and even if they like someone who is not treating them the way they deserve, they will still walk away. They don't compromise their standards for someone else and they know what kind of person they *deserve* to be with.

2. They're not afraid of speaking up.

They're not afraid to tell someone what they did wrong or call someone out on their lies. This is why they're often labeled *'intimidating'* because they can stand up for themselves and will not hold back.

3. They don't 'need' a man.

They crave love and affection but they will never need a man to complete them. Love will always be a *choice* to them; not something they're looking for out of fear of being alone or getting old. They're content with their own lives and love is a sweet addition not a necessity.

4. They know how to move on.

They've learned how to move on when they have to. They will never be the ones to beg someone to stay with them or beg for a second chance. They're confident that they will be fine and that they will find someone better.

5. They don't allow themselves to be options.

Strong women will not tolerate being treated like an option or being part of a bunch of women someone is dating. They appreciate commitment and honesty and anything other than that is a deal breaker for them.

6. They don't play by the 'rules.'

In life or in love, don't expect strong women to follow any dating practices you're used to or play it safe. They will surprise you by how daring and bold they are and they will never shy away from anything they truly want.

7. They know how to handle rejection.

They're not afraid of the word 'no,' they've heard it before and they will continue to hear it but that doesn't stop them from trying, strong women face more rejections because they actually go out and ask for what they want instead of waiting for things to come to them and the more risks they take, the more rejections they'll face, but these rejections only make them stronger.

8. They ask the hard questions.

They will ask the questions men like to evade, they will ask where they stand and where things are going, they will ask to meet your family and friends and be involved in your life. Strong women are passionate and curious in all aspects of their lives and dating is no exception.

9. They've been heartbroken before.

Even though they act like they're unbreakable, they've fallen in love and gotten heartbroken before, heartbreak only made them wiser but not *indifferent*. They still have a lot of love to give, they just need to know who is worthy of it and who is just playing with their hearts.

10. They don't look for validation from others.

Strong women look for validation from their success, their work, their friendships and how they lead their lives. They know that the right person will find them when the time is right and they don't let their relationship status define their worth or define them.

4

Strong Women Don't Fall In Love

Heidi Priebe

Strong women don't fall in love.

They tread in love. Strong women entertain love, they flirt with it, they embody it with caution and they escape from it unscathed. Everyone knows that. Only weak women allow love to affect them. Strong women couldn't care less.

Strong women live their lives alone.

They may have flings or fuck buddies or even domestic partnerships but never, ever lovers. Love makes you crippled and small. Love stops you from achieving what you want out of life. Strong women don't fall in love because love is an emotion. And real women do not feel anything pervasively. Real women switch their sentiments on and off like a light switch. Real women are strong because they have mastered detachment. And detachment is the ultimate end goal.

Anyone else tired of hearing these tirades?

Because I am. I am tired—and I don't think I'm alone—of the

infinite set of contradictions we set up for each other. The criticism we face when we love, the criticism we face when we don't. I am tired of being told what is strong and what is weak. What is right and what is wrong. What we ought to feel and what we ought to talk about. We are scathed for being loveless and burned for being honest about what we want. We can't win this game. And I'd like to encourage us all to stop playing.

Strong has nothing to do with detachment. Strong has nothing to do with your track record. Strong has nothing to do with how fast or how often or how successfully you fall in and out of love. Strong is a measure of the integrity that you bring to your life. And that means that you're the one calling the shots.

Strong means knowing what you want. Strong means fighting like hell for the life that you want to be living, whether the end goal is getting elected as president or staying home to raise a family. Strong means living by your own definition. Strong means ignoring anyone who belittles your struggles as you fight to live a life that you're proud of. Strong means you're walking in line with whatever it is that you believe in.

I believe in love. And I believe in my own strength. For me, those things walk hand in hand—and they have to. The people who scoff at attachment, who praise disengagement, who pride themselves on being independent to the point of unattainability, will never understand the immense amount of strength it takes to love. To expose your vulnerabilities. To put your heart and your desires on the line without any guarantee of reciprocation. My definition of strength is risking everything I have because I know that I can put myself back together once it's over.

I know that you can be sad and also strong.

You can be scared and also strong.

I know that you can be putting your life back together—piece by painstaking piece and still be an absolute mountain. You get to set your definition of strength. And you get to live by it every single day of your life.

'Strong women don't fall in love' is utter bullshit. And it's a story that we've got to stop telling ourselves. Strong women accept themselves. Strong women understand themselves. Strong women show up to every last moment of their lives, whether it's painful or triumphant or impossible. Strong women are blazing with glory and strong women are getting trampled on down in the arena. They are not a single, hard shell that never gets broken. Strong women are beaten down and built back up a thousand times more often than each weak person who sits on the bleachers and judges their choices.

It takes no strength to avoid your life. It takes no gusto to criticize others. It takes no effort to hide away and deny yourself the things that you want out of life because you're scared that somebody is going to call you weak. What takes strength is showing up. What takes strength is being present. What takes strength is admitting what you want from your life and moving towards it without a regard for anyone else's opinion.

Strong women fall in love. Strong women don't. Strong women work high-powered jobs. Strong women stay at home. Strong women live by no single, meek definition of the word and they have only one thing in common—they decided the life that they wanted. And they went for it.

Strong women set their own rules. And that's the only definition that matters.

5

11 Things Strong Fathers Teach Their Daughters About How To Be A Strong Woman

Nicole Tarkoff

1. Always put your best effort forward, and when that's not enough, keep trying.

Strong fathers teach their daughters that hard work is never easy; it is exhausting; it is demanding; it is all-encompassing, but he teaches her that effort is rewarding, even if it isn't tangible. Her determination is relentless, and she gets it from her father.

2. Be able to stand on your own.

A strong father teaches his strong daughter to rely on herself first. She's learned that independence is a wonderful thing to have, but she's also learned that needing help is not a weakness, and asking for it demonstrates strength. She can stand on her own, but she has the ability to lean on others when her own balance fails her.

3. It's okay to fail.

She knows the expense of expectation when it comes to being raised by a strong father, but she knows that occasional failure is not only acceptable, it's inevitable. Failure is a side effect of trying, and strong daughters are not contained by the fear of failure. She sees failure as an opportunity to try again because her father has taught her to do so.

4. Respect yourself.

He teaches his daughter to respect her body, her mind, her thoughts, her instincts. He teaches her to respect herself enough to walk away from those who hurt her, to accept the love he has shown her she deserves, and she does.

5. Believe in yourself.

He tells her that her dreams are valid, and to not let anyone make her feel otherwise. He tells her to believe in herself the way he believes in her. Strong fathers know that their daughters can achieve anything they set their mind to.

6. Place your happiness first.

He teaches her that loving yourself is not selfish, it's necessary.

He tells her to find happiness within herself before she goes searching for it everywhere else. Because all the outer places she finds happiness may lead to disappointment, but no one can take away the happiness she alone creates, and this is the kind of happiness that she should share with others. He teaches her that this is the kind of happiness that lasts.

7. You will always be loved.

There are more kinds of love than romantic love, stronger kinds. The bond a strong daughter and father share endures. When her heart feels broken or she feels undeserving of love, he reassures her she's surrounded by it every day.

8. Relationships take work, all kinds: platonic, romantic, familial.

He teaches her that not everyone will always agree with her. There will be arguments, grudges, times when communication and understanding is flawed, but the important relationships, the ones that matter, the ones with people who love her, people who want the best for her, are worth every bit of effort she puts into them.

9. Trust your gut; your instinct is important.

She knows when to listen to the inner voice telling her something's not right. She knows how to trust herself, and her intuition. A strong father teaches his daughter that her feelings aren't wrong, or illegitimate, they're indicative of her ability to understand herself, her wants, her needs, her fears, her aspirations, everything in life that matters to her.

10. Always take pride in your accomplishments.

She knows humility, but she is proud of every success she's ever had, and she won't let anyone take that away from her. He teaches her to own her intelligence, to not let others undermine it. He teaches her to expose her strengths and never dim them.

11. Know your father's love will always be with you.

A strong father teaches his daughter that his love is eternal. His love gives her strength. A strong daughter always carries her father's love with her.

6

The Truth About Being A Strong Woman

Marisa Donnelly

This is what an anonymous man wrote to me just the other day: *Being strong is not rewarded. Women are expected to be vulnerable. Being strong means that you're inevitably bitter or jaded about something, and that's just not attractive.*

Here is what being a strong woman means to me: It means standing up for myself. It means that I am a fully-functioning human, one who is independent and able to do things for herself. It means that I have opinions and beliefs that I stand for, and that I do not settle for less.

It doesn't mean that I don't ask for help. I do (often). Asking for help doesn't mean I'm weak, it means I'm able to acknowledge that I'm not a super woman, and that I'm going to need other people sometimes.

Being strong doesn't mean that I close myself off from others and act like I'm better than them. (Actually, I'm always striving to be better, live better, love better, which is about *me* rather than anyone else.) It doesn't mean that I force my beliefs down other people's throats or judge them for how they think. It doesn't mean that I'm 'inevitably bitter or jaded.' In fact, a strong woman is a woman who loves herself and her world and is therefore positive, loving, and self-assured.

To be a strong woman simply means that I am grounded and confident in who I am.

I read this man's comment. Then read it again. And resisted the incredible urge to reply and start a back-and-forth battle via computer screens that would end up going nowhere. But even after a few days, this comment has stayed with me.

See, this is the misconception about strong women: we are difficult to love. But in all reality, it's the complete opposite. **Strong women are the best women to love.** We are the women with fierce compassion. We know who we are and we are not afraid to embrace that. **We love whole-heartedly because we love ourselves.** And we are not only looking to better ourselves, but our partners, our worlds. If you're a man that's intimidated by a strong woman, perhaps it is because you know this woman will push you to be better, will make you see the world differently, will challenge you.

Another misconception about strong women is that we're incapable of being vulnerable. The funny thing is: **to be strong, you first have to be vulnerable.** You have to look yourself straight in the eye and acknowledge all the parts of yourself that need improvement, all the parts of you that you try to hide behind a smiling face.

Vulnerability means being brutally honest with yourself; it

means setting aside your pride and being open with someone and letting them in. Do not mistake independence and strength with an inability to let someone in. A woman that is confident with herself is a woman that will face love straight on. **She is a woman that can be vulnerable in a relationship because she knows who she is.** And she will let her significant other discover that person by peeling back those layers, together.

The truth about being a strong woman is that the world sees us as a threat. We're just 'too much', 'too intimidating', too 'jaded' and 'miserable' and 'bitter'. But we are none of those things. We are women with backbones. Women who aren't afraid to be proud of ourselves in a world that might not always support us. Women who know the value of our vulnerability, our passion, our strength. And women who will fight any anonymous man who dares to say we should be any other way.

7

When The Perpetually Single Girl Craves Love

Becca Martin

She's prided herself for so long on being single, on being perfectly fine on her own, because she is. She's not single because no one wants her; she isn't unwanted or incapable of love. She just hasn't found someone to make her heart skip a beat. She hasn't found someone that fills her stomach with butterflies at the sight of them. She hasn't found someone she misses before they're even gone. She hasn't found someone to make her want to give up being single because her happiness was born in her decision to be single.

She loves being on her own; she has become her own saving grace and her own backbone. She's gone through loss, fights, hard times and good times without a S/O by her side. She's tough and she's been tough for others. She stands up for herself and makes sure she gets treated the way she deserves.

She doesn't need someone to complete her or fix her. She is whole on her own; she has filled her own voids, figured out how to fix things on her own. She can carry her own weight on her shoulders and she's proud of it.

She's found herself and she loves herself.

She's gotten used to being single, maybe a little to used to it. She's become comfortable with it, maybe a little too comfortable with it.

There are times she gets lonely because life isn't meant to be lived alone all the time. Even though she can do things for herself, on her own, doesn't necessarily means she always wants to.

There are times when—even though she can carry all her groceries inside in two loads—sometimes she'd rather have someone there to help her do it in one. There are times that instead of putting air in her own tires sometimes she'd like someone to do it for her. There are times that she would rather share the grill with someone instead of always grilling her own burgers.

There are times that instead of coming home to an empty house and cooking dinner for herself she would rather be cooking dinner for someone else. There are times that she would rather be waking up to someone she loves instead of waking up alone. There are times she would rather cook breakfast for two, make coffee for two and have someone to share her mornings with.

Because as strong, as independent, as happy as she is on her own sometimes she just needs a hand to hold. Someone to kiss her when she's feeling down, someone to tell her she looks beautiful when she's doubting herself, someone to be goofy when she's upset because as great as being single is, it isn't better than love.

Even the perpetually single girl craves love, craves attention and craves the feeling of being wanted. As much as she craves it, it isn't that easy to find. There have been guys who have come and gone, guys who haven't stuck around, and guys who broke her heart, so she started being guarded. She started choosing herself, she started putting herself first and before she realized it she started becoming happier that way.

She started finding happiness in herself, she stopped getting let down, she stopped getting her heart broken. She became strong and it led her to where she is now, but even the perpetually single girl craves love because it's a long trip alone.

8

Sometimes The Girl Who Is Always There For Everyone Else, Needs Someone There For Her

Bianca Sparacino

When you're the girl who is always there for others, you feel a lot. You have depths within you, an ocean for a heart, and you keep falling for people who are too scared to swim. You give and you give and you give; tearing pieces of your paper soul into the smallest of fragments just to set someone else aflame.

You hurt. My God, do you hurt. You ache, wondering if someone will ever give you the love you so freely give to others, wondering if there will come a time when someone asks how you are doing, how you are coping, how you are healing.

And when that doesn't happen, you heal yourself. You find strength in things other than people. You find energy in your solitude; you find hope in your daydreams. You build yourself up, tell yourself that you don't need anyone to save you, that you don't need anyone to steady your foundation.

But you do.

See, sometimes the girl who is always there for everyone else needs someone there for her. Sometimes, the girl who smiles the biggest holds the biggest hurt. Sometimes the girl who is always the person who wipes the tears of others, goes home and cries lakes into the midnight hour. Sometimes the girl who encourages everyone around her needs to be told that she is appreciated, that she matters; sometimes she needs to be encouraged herself.

So if you're the girl who is always there for others, know that your heart is rare. Know that you hold within you an ability to calm storms in people, a beautiful gift that has relieved sore eyes and hurt minds. Know that you give people hope, that you inspire them by acknowledging the pieces of them most ignore, that you make people feel wanted, that you make people feel like they have purpose.

However, also remind yourself that you are not invincible. Your heart needs rest. You need rest. Remind yourself that you do not need to carry the weight of the world on your shoulders, that you may not be able to save everyone, that you may not be able to heal every hurt. Remind yourself that you deserve to take all of the energy you put out into the world and invest it back into yourself from time to time. That you are worthy of the love you keep giving to everyone else. Remind yourself that you don't always have to be strong, that you don't always have to be the fixer. Remind yourself that you can be human, that you can ask for help, and that you don't always have to be the one to save yourself.

9

Here's To The Girls Who Are A Lot To Handle

Kendra Syrdal

Here's to the girls who are a lot to handle.

Who are loud and unapologetic. Who laugh without worrying if someone is taking a picture and they have a double chin and laugh lines. Who speak their minds without giving a second thought about the reaction of whoever hears. Who say what they want and never ask for permission if it feels right. Who speak from the heart and know that's a good thing.

Here's to the girls who are a bit too much.

Who wear their hearts on their sleeves and do not apologize for bleeding on your shirt when you cross paths. Who say what they mean and mean what they say. Who do not hide behind "playing games" and "just talking" and "no labels." Who ask for what they need even if it's difficult to swallow.

Here's to the girls who are "not like other girls."

Who reject that headline because, what the fuck does it even mean. Who don't worry about their femininity being this or that, here nor there, enough or not enough. Who don't worry about being like anyone else just because of a vagina and simply do them. Who are who they are and nothing else and no label can ever express that.

Here's to the girls who can't be tamed.

Who are absolutely unconcerned with fitting into a box just because a boyfriend or a girlfriend or a partner or their parents or society has told them it's where they belong. Who choose to run, and if someone runs along with them it's a blessing but not a requirement. Who live their lives with freedom and fire and do not worry about bothering anyone with the heat.

Here's to the the girls who defy expectations.

Who do not wait for a ring on their finger or a relationship status on Facebook because they know it's the least interesting thing about them. Who do what they want with their bodies and pay no mind to words like "slut" or "whore" or "ladylike" because they know those words hold no weight. Who decide to be quieter and selective and refuse to give value to words like "prude" or "uptight" or "boring" because they know how little words from uninformed places matter. Who are unequivocally themselves.

Here's to the girls who choose to be whoever they want to be.

Who cheers with beer or champagne or apple juice or water but cheers loudly and enthusiastically because they are excited about the possibility of simply being themselves. Who march and skip and toss their hair whether it's styled or not even brushed because they know, they KNOW that they are *fabulous*. That they are amazing. That they are worthy. That they are strong.

Here's to the girls who refuse to listen to the hate.

Who see it, narrow their eyes at it, and then shake, shake, shake it off because they know it doesn't matter. Who only give value to constructive criticism but never give anything to hateful, antagonistic actions. Who refuse to pay attention to people who are only interested in the idea of bringing a women, a *strong* woman, to the ground. Who, when hearing the people saying stop, say "No!" and keep on dancing.

Here's to the girls who are wild and free.

Who have lived through whatever, battled whatever, faced whatever, and choose to power on. Who look at the chains that could hold them down, would hold others down, and choose to run regardless. Who see the lists of things they're supposed to be and decide that the only person who can decide to give them a "supposed to" is them. Who reject weights and in turn accept wings. Who see melancholy, and choose magic. Who see sadness, and choose something else.

Here's to the girls who are a lot to handle.

Who go home alone because no one else can deal with not holding, or having to hold, your hand. Who ask for what they need and do not make excuses because a why isn't part of a request. Who are who they are because they love who they are and they refuse to settle for anyone who cannot love them as completely.

Here's to the girls who are a lot to handle.

You *aren't* a lot to handle. You're magnificent.
You *aren't* a lot to handle. You're just fine.
You *aren't* a lot to handle. You're just YOU.

And I see you.
And I am with you.
And I *am* you.

And I love you.

10

15 Reminders For Anyone Who Wants To Date A Woman Who Has Been Put Through Hell

Brianna Wiest

1. She's more resilient than you can fathom, which means she won't put up with your bullshit for too long. People who have been through hell know that they are capable of moving on.

2. If she seems like she's overanalyzing what you say, it's because in the past, those offhand comments were warning signs that she brushed off too easily.

3. If it seems like she's overthinking your relationship, it's because in the past, she learned not to always trust what she feels.

4. She doesn't tell you about her past because she's broken or because it still bothers her. She tells you because doing so is a form of intimacy.

5. If you feel the urge to call her "crazy," consider how you would have responded had you been put in the same circumstances that she was. Chances are, she reacted as any human being with the capacity to feel would. If she weren't "crazy," she'd be an emotionless psychopath. She would have been okay with how she was treated.

6. Be glad she wasn't okay with how she was treated.

7. There will be some things that trigger her, or at least remind her of past experiences. Let those be moments in which you reassure her that this is different. If it doesn't bring you closer, it will push you farther apart.

8. Know what you want before you ask her out. Don't win her trust, open her heart and spend time with her only to tell her it's "not the right time." All she will hear is: "You are not the right person."

9. Be consistently straightforward. It's different from being blunt, and it's even more different from being honest once in a while.

10. The fine line between being honest and being hurtful is taking a pause to ask yourself: "Is this something that she needs to know? What benefit is there in telling her this very honest thing?"

11. Don't confuse silence for acceptance. Sometimes battles have to be chosen, that doesn't mean she isn't noticing everything.

12. Don't confuse forgiveness for forgetting. People who have been through a lot do not forget when someone gives them a glimpse at their true character.

13. Remind her that the only way to see whether or not relationship will work is by being it. The quality of love is not the median of all the thoughts you have about it; you can't think your way into partnership. You either do or don't. Actions are everything.

14. You do not need to be the idea of a "perfect partner." You don't have to be perfect at all. What she's looking for is genuine connection, and the kind of person who will protect and nurture that connection when they find it.

15. Understand that she is the person she is because of what she went through. Don't see her as a victim with baggage, see her as a survivor who still—miraculously—has the capacity to love.

11

10 Things You Learn From Being Raised By A Strong Mother

Rania Naim

1. You learn the value of independence.

You don't need a man to save you or anyone to take care of you, you learn by example that you are capable of living a full and happy life without having to share it with someone else. You learn that you can build a home, raise kids, cook, and do the dishes all while having a thriving career. You pretty much learn how to be super woman.

2. You learn the meaning of unconditional love.

You saw your mom sacrifice her time, health and youth for you and your siblings, yet she never complained or gloated about how much she is suffering or how much she is doing. She always had a smile on her face and was happily giving more and more of herself. She taught you what selfless and unconditional love looks like, and you know you won't be able to find that love anywhere else.

3. You learn how to love yourself.

You learn how to walk away from the things that are not meant for you, you learn how to keep going even when the whole world is against you, and you learn how to believe in yourself when everyone is doubting you. You learn that bad grades, heart breaks and failures don't define you; what defines you is how you bounce back from all the setbacks and how hard you fight for the life you want.

4. You learn that you can be both strong and soft.

Strong mothers are usually very sensitive they just hide it better, but you saw your mom silently cry over your pain, or stay up all night taking care of you when you were sick, or the nights she couldn't sleep because something was troubling you. The way she hugs you when you are down shows unmatched compassion and tenderness and sometimes in a quiet corner you saw her shed a few tears.

5. You learn that it's not easy being a woman.

You learn that your opinion will be discounted, that you will be taken lightly when you're being serious, but you will also learn that you can stand out in a crowd and force everyone to listen to your voice and accept your ideas. You learn that what doesn't kill you makes you stronger.

6. You learn never to look back.

You learn to let all the "what ifs" and "could have beens" go. You learn not to look back and wonder why life turned upside down. You just keep looking forward and let the past redeem itself. You learn that everything that happened got you to where you belong even if it is nothing you ever wished for.

7. You learn the importance of patience and faith.

You learn that God is looking out for you and your struggles, that everything will be OK in the end. Storms will pass and tomorrow is a new day. You learn to be patient with life, patient with timing, patient with success and patient with problems. You learn that *patience is strength*.

8. You learn how to create your own happiness.

You can find happiness in a difficult life. You can still be happy even if you are carrying the weight of the world on your shoulders. My mom taught me that I can always find something to smile about all I have to do is look closer.

9. You learn that she still knows more about love than you do.

Even when you are generations apart, even if you are not fond of her love choices, if she doesn't approve of someone you better listen to her. She knows what she is saying; moreover, she doesn't want to see you get heartbroken. As much as I hate to admit it, she got it right every time.

10. You learn how to be a good mother.

You've been raised by a mom who showed you how to truly take care of a family, who showed you that hard work pays off, who showed you that you can love someone unconditionally. She showed you how to be protective, loving, kind, compassionate, strong and resilient. She was leading by example, and whether you know it or not, you are following in her footsteps one step at a time.

12

Strong Women Are Allowed To Break Down Too

Lauren Jarvis-Gibson

A strong woman is not a body full of steel. She is full of washed down tears, settled dust, a bruised heart, and cells that still ache from time to time. She has spent years with a heavy weight on her shoulders. She has spent years with tears that slide down her red cheeks with no one there to catch them.

But make no mistake, she is anything but weak. Because she still goes about her days lifting all of that weight.

She lets her tears fall on the ground, watering the flowers as she goes.

She doesn't play the victim. She doesn't bend with the sadness that likes to surround her heart. She stands tall. **Despite the weight, and despite the grief, she stands tall.**

A strong woman doesn't let grief keep her down for long. But the strongest women are the ones who call for help when they know they need it. They never hide behind their curtains to hide the sun from their eyes. They don't fake their way to the top. They call for help when they are hurting because they know they can't do everything on their own even if they want to. **They know that sometimes it's ok to not be ok.**

Strong women are allowed to break down. They are allowed to fall from the big bags of sadness they carry with their shoulders. They stumble. They cry out. They sink to the ground. Because they know that they are allowed to do it. They know that they can't carry so much at one time. And that sometimes, they need to let it all go. **They need to take the weight off.**

Strong women ask for help. They don't wait until the last second. They don't reapply their makeup after crying all night. They let their true self shine, no matter what it looks like. They know that they can't hide from themselves.

And they know it takes strength to break down. It takes bravery to crumble.

Strong women break down. They suffer. They hurt. But they always ask for guidance. They always ask for help.

And when their wounds have been bandaged up and the scab is finally almost gone, they get back up.

They let go of that baggage. And they continue to walk on their journey. To smile through the sadness. To be confident in themselves, and confident that they will get through anything. No matter what. Even through the break downs. They will make it.

13

22 Empowering Quotes From Kickass Women About How Women Kick Ass

Jessica Winters

1. "You can be the king, but watch the queen conquer."
—Nicki Minaj

2. "A girl should be two things: who and what she wants."
—Coco Chanel

3. "'I am not an angel,' I asserted; 'and I will not be one till I die: I will be myself.'"
—Charlotte Brontë

4. "If I follow the inclination of my nature, it is this: beggar-woman and single, far rather than queen and married."
—Queen Elizabeth I

5. "A woman with a strong sense of personal power is self-confident enough to accurately identify her strengths as well as her blind spots, which she is continually working to improve."

—Stacey Radin

6. "Be the woman who is remembered for living life to its fullest!"

—Erin Fall Haskell

7. "Women are leaders everywhere you look—from the CEO who runs a Fortune 500 company to the housewife who raises her children and heads her household. Our country was built by strong women, and we will continue to break down walls and defy stereotypes."

—Nancy Pelosi

8. "All women are a reflection, a mirror of the Goddess. Remember...you are the Universe figuring itself out. So of course you are identical to the female aspect of divinity."

—Robin Rumi

9. "I'm single because I was born that way."

—Mae West

10. "I hate men who are afraid of women's strength."

—Anaïs Nin

11. "I do not wish them [women] to have power over men; but over themselves."

—Mary Wollstonecraft

12. "There are some who want to get married and others who don't. I have never had an impulse to go to the altar. I am a difficult person to lead."

—Greta Garbo

13. "We need to reshape our own perception of how we view ourselves. We have to step up as women and take the lead."

—Beyoncé

14. "If you want something said, ask a man; if you want something done, ask a woman."

—Margaret Thatcher

15. "The thing women have yet to learn is nobody gives you power. You just take it."

—Roseanne Barr

16. "A woman is like a tea bag—you never know how strong she is until she gets in hot water."

—Eleanor Roosevelt

17. "We need women at all levels, including the top, to change the dynamic, reshape the conversation, to make sure women's voices are heard and heeded, not overlooked and ignored."

—Sheryl Sandberg

18. "I myself have never able to find out precisely what a feminist is. I only know that people call me a feminist whenever I express sentiments that differentiate me from a doormat."

—*Rebecca West*

19. "A strong woman understands that the gifts such as logic, decisiveness, and strength are just as feminine as intuition and emotional connection. She values and uses all of her gifts."

—*Nancy Rathburn*

20. "Every woman that finally figured out her worth, has picked up her suitcases of pride and boarded a flight to freedom, which landed in the valley of change."

—*Shannon L. Alder*

21. "Women are the real architects of society."

—*Harriet Beecher Stowe*

22. "I am a Woman Phenomenally. Phenomenal Woman, that's me."

—*Maya Angelou*

14

This Is How A Self-Assured Woman Loves Differently

Kim Quindlen

She trusts herself most of all, enough to know that she would never choose to be with someone who didn't deserve her. She does not love arrogantly, but she does love with the expectation that she will be treated well, respected, and supported as much as she will do the same for her partner. She has worked hard to finally love herself—to take her flaws with her strengths, to believe she is deserving of happiness, to be comfortable in her own skin. She has worked hard to gain the confidence that allows her to focus on her own story and abstain from comparing it to everyone else's around her.

And when she looks for love, she looks for someone who can continue on this path with her, on the path to loving yourself. Because she has learned that once you can do that, your heart has so much more room to love others even more deeply.

She loves daringly and freely. She is still very much afraid of pain, but she's had enough dark days to understand that

they always end, that she always makes it out on the other side.

She knows who she is outside of her relationship, she knows that she is whole entirely, without her partner. Which is why it is so easy for her to fall into love and to allow it to consume her in the best way possible. She's not afraid to be vulnerable, because even if things fall apart, she knows how to put herself back together. She knows how to be by herself, she knows how to enjoy her own company. She knows that her life still has meaning and purpose outside of the one she loves, even if she loves them above all else. That is why she continues to give her heart out to those she knows will take care of it.

She understands the difference between preferences and necessities in a partner. Maybe she'd greatly enjoy dating a tall man or a petite woman, but when it comes down to the heart of it, she knows that all of those things are just bonuses—that what she really needs in a partner is emotional connection, mutual encouragement, unwavering loyalty, or whatever else it is that is intensely important to her. She has felt passion and infatuation many times over, sometimes so much so that she could practically taste the feeling. But she understands the difference between infatuation and love. She understands the experiences that are fleetingly addictive, and the ones that are unbroken, substantial, and made to last long after the initial high.

She is not angry, suspicious, or insecure in her relationships. She's been through enough and seen enough to trust

her gut instinct. She knows that there is a right way to feel pain in love and a wrong way to feel pain in love.

She knows that the right way comes with the knowledge that this person has their hand wrapped around your heart, that you trust them enough to be gentle with it, and that you know that fully loving them means giving in to the fact that if anything ever happened to them, you'd be broken for a long time. She knows that the wrong way to feel pain comes when someone hurts you over and over again, even if it's unintentional, because they value their own comfort and security above your happiness. She does not toy around with these kinds of relationships. When she feels the wrong kind of pain, she walks away, no matter how much she doesn't want to.

She is drawn to challenge. Not in a sexual-tension-filled, prime-time drama kind of way. But in the way that promises that the person she chooses will continue to inspire her, stretch her, and dare her for the rest of her life. She wants someone who sees unlimited potential within her, and someone who treats her with tenderness without ever thinking of her as fragile.

But most of all, she loves fiercely. She loves with a spark. She believes that walls are cowardly and love is brave. She'd risk pain rather than sleep safely in the corner. She keeps her eyes wide and her heart wider. She loves in the way that she knows best. All you have to do is deserve her.

15

For The Women Who Feel Like 'Too Much'

Heidi Priebe

For the women who feel like 'too much'—you know exactly who you are.

You're the ones who grew up always feeling different—feeling crazy, feeling brash, feeling just a little too passionate and fierce. You're the ones who've spent your whole lives being told to bite your tongue, to sit on your hands, to settle down and shut up and quell your restless mind for just long enough to blend in.

To find your place within the calmer, cooler crowds.

You're the ones who've always struggled to regulate your spirit. The ones who've felt the pull between the wild and the tame—the never-ending yearning to go and yet the underlying longing to stay. The constant need to explore further and yet the quiet desire to settle down.

You're the ones who can't find peace within yourself. Who have always wanted to try harder, run faster, push yourself further than the world around you ever expected you to go.

You're the ones with the expectations so high that even you can never live up to yourself. Even you can sometimes find your mind to be 'too much' for your body.

And yet you're also the one who's irreplaceable.

You're the one who may always be a little too passionate, a little too reckless and too intense.

But you're also the one who loves the hardest. Who fights the longest. Who refuses to cash in her chips and give up when the rest of the crowd has laid their swords down and gone home.

You're the one who keeps pushing for the changes that need making. Who won't sit down or shut up or settle down when what the stakes are rising higher than you're ready for. You're the one who's not afraid to stand up when the rest of the world is staying silent.

You're the one who may always be 'too much' for the people who are calm and complacent and steady.

But you'll never be too much for the fierce ones.

You'll never be too much for the ones who burn as brightly, who reel as wildly, who move as quickly as you.

You'll never be too much for the people who want to experience the whole of life fully—arms wide open and spirit braced for whatever's coming their way. You will always be *just the right amount* for the people who's fire matches your own.

But there's a catch-22 when it comes to finding them.

Because they're not the ones sitting down. Shutting up. And listening to what they have been told their entire life to do.

They are the ones running ahead of the pack.

And if it's not too much for you to handle, it is up to you to run and catch up.

Thought Catalog, it's a website.

www.thoughtcatalog.com

Social

facebook.com/thoughtcatalog
twitter.com/thoughtcatalog
tumblr.com/thoughtcatalog
instagram.com/thoughtcatalog

Corporate

www.thought.is